Open your heart, spread love

10. Inhale
Urdvha Hastasana
Upward Hands Pose

Begin & End
Stand Tall, Feet together, Hands together on your chest and invite the sun to shine in to your heart

9. Exhale
Uttanasana
Forward Fold

8. Inhale
Uttanasana
Forward Fold

6. Inhale
Urdvha Mukha Svanasana
Upward Facing Dog

7. Exhale
Adho Mukha Svanasana
Downward Facing Dog

You can repeat it 3-5 times. While practicing the poses, focus on expressing gratitude for love, light and peace which shines like sun, within yourself and others around you.

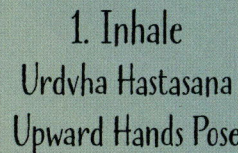

1. Inhale
Urdvha Hastasana
Upward Hands Pose

2. Exhale
Uttanasana
Forward Fold

3. Inhale
Ardha Uttanasana
Half Forward Fold

5. Exhale continued
Chatturunga Dandasana
Four Limb Staff Pose

4. Exhale
Kumbhakasana
Plank Pose

In the mornings, when the sun opens his eyes, he shines his love and light on everyone equally and unconditionally. He believes the power of love that he carries, is infinite and higher than any other power.

Reyhan
A passenger of the Yoga journey and the writer of "Water, Wisdom and Love" book for adults.

Instagram:
@Orangefeather_art_yoga
@Water_wisdom_and_love